FAITH MOMENTS

FINDING STRENTGH IN GOD'S WORD WHEN LIFE DOESN'T MAKE SENSE

A.B. VINES

Faith Moments

Finding Strength in God's Word When Life Doesn't Make Sense

Copyright © 2025 by A. B. Vines

AUTHOR'S CONTACT

+1(619)726-4976

Dedication v

Acknowledgment vi

About the Author vii

Foreword ix

Introduction xii

The Blessedness of Each Day 1

The Brevity of Life 6

The Power of Your Tongue 14

The Power of Encouragement 22

Attentiveness and Action on God's Word 29

Don't Quit Yet! 34

The Three Pillars of Life 38

How to Have a Great Day 46

The "Acts" of Dealing with People 53

Avoid the Pit of Anger 60

Maintain an Attitude of Thankfulness 66

Winning Spiritual Warfare 73

The Happiness of the World Versus the Joy of the Lord
.... 79

Maintain Spiritual Alertness 84

The Faithfulness of God 90

Table of Contents

The Power of Humility 96

Have a Mindset of Victory..101

Reaping the Fruits of Your Labor...............................107

Value Relationship Above Service 112

He Lives Among Us...117

Wisdom for Greatness...122

Table of Contents

Dedication

This book is a testament to my deep love and unwavering dedication to my family. It is dedicated to my late father, Johnny Lee Vines, and my mother, the late Bettie Ruth Vines, my ultimate hero.

I also dedicate it to my inspiring aunts, Gloria Gene Robinson and Joyce Maria Ruffin. Furthermore, this work is dedicated to the joy and pain of my life, my children Latoya, Brandon AJ, Jasmine, and Shane. This dedication is a reflection of the love and appreciation I have for each of you, my dear family members.

Finally, it is a dedication to the love of my life, 1st Lady Karen Vines (a Philly Girl), who is the greatest gift in my life besides my salvation in Jesus Christ.

Acknowledgment

My foremost appreciation goes to God Almighty for the inspiration and wisdom He gave to me to come up with the idea of FAITH MOMENTS.

I also want to sincerely thank and appreciate all the members of New Seasons Church for their consistent support and love. None of these feats of mine would have been possible without you all. Your faith in me has made me better, and I will always be grateful for your love and trust.

I might not be able to mention your names individually, but I deeply appreciate your individual and collective roles in my church family. God bless you all for me in Jesus's name, Amen.

About the Author

A.B. Vines, Sr., D.Min., with his over thirty years of experience in ministry, has served as a preacher, teacher, and pastor at New Seasons Church in Spring Valley, CA. His leadership has significantly impacted ministries locally and nationally.

In 2016, the Elders of New Seasons Church established the New Seasons Global Network to acknowledge the church's increasing influence. This network acts as a central point for leadership and ministry oversight. That same year, A.B. Vines was consecrated as a Bishop in the Lord's Church, receiving unanimous approval from the General Board of the Church of God in Christ, Inc., under the guidance of the late Honorable Bishop George Dallas McKinney.

After his consecration, Bishop Vines assumed pivotal roles in ministry, being elected as the 1st Vice President of the Southern Baptist Convention and as President of the California Southern Baptist Convention. Under his visionary leadership, the church's impact has significantly expanded across California, Georgia, Indiana, Africa, and Haiti, giving us hope for a brighter future.

First Lady Karen Vines and her husband are parents to five, grandparents to thirteen, and great-grandparents to two. Bishop Vines is committed to fulfilling his mission of **R**eaching, **E**quipping, **I**nspiring, **G**rowing, **A**nd **N**urturing God's people to fulfill their destiny.

This book is a testament to my deep love and unwavering dedication to my family. It is dedicated to my late father, Johnny Lee Vines, and my mother, the late Bettie Ruth Vines, my ultimate hero. I also dedicate it to my inspiring aunts, Gloria Gene Robinson and Joyce Maria Ruffin. Furthermore, this work is dedicated to the joy and pain of my life, my children Latoya, Brandon AJ, Jasmine, and Shane. This dedication is a reflection of the love and appreciation I have for each of you, my dear family members. Finally, it is a dedication to the love of my life, 1st Lady Karen Vines (a Philly Girl), who is the greatest gift in my life besides my salvation in Jesus Christ.

P.S. I want to sincerely thank New Seasons Church for their consistent support. None of this would be possible without you. Your faith in me has made me better, and I will always be grateful for your love and trust. I deeply appreciate each and every one of you in my church family.

Foreword

When the Christian life is, in any way, drained or sanitized of devotion and love, it becomes utterly burdensome. It morphs into a lifeless, heartless pursuit of self-improvement and self-discipline. It becomes a monotonous routine, fraught with either failure and self-loathing, or self-created success and religious arrogance. It becomes a "machine that runs you" rather than a relationship to which you run! Ultimately, this kind of "Christianity" kills your heart.

A relationship with Jesus Christ is something completely different! Christianity is supposed to be a life-giving, grace-enjoying, joy-producing, strength-renewing journey that draws you into close fellowship with Jesus and undergirds you through every hardship of life. This journey is supposed to be delightful beyond comprehension. It should be stabilizing through every life-circumstance and transforming in a way that no self-effort can produce. Knowing Jesus gives you an identity that cannot be damaged, a love that cannot be taken away, and a a grace that will carry you until you seen Him.

He is the pursuit. He is the prize. He is attractive, lovable, and altogether wonderful!

Yet, how often, along the journey, do we lose our devotion. We lose our first love. We wander off the path of passionate relationship only to find ourselves seemingly lost in a fog of performance-based acceptance and self-effort. From this place, the Christian life seems like a ladder taller than I could ever climb! It feels, eventually hopeless.

In these pages, Bishop A.B. Vines has wonderfully invited every believer back to the foundation of devotion to Jesus. He compels you to personally and intimately pursue Jesus Christ in an ongoing relationship. In so doing, he gives you the key to enjoying your Christian life faithfully for the duration. He gives you the path to experiencing the true personal transformation and spiritual growth for which you long. It all flows from loving Jesus and walking with Him personally. The abundant Christian life is hiding in your personal, private walk with Jesus as Saviour and Friend.

As I read these pages, I was challenged to deepen my devotion to the Saviour I love. I was reminded about what attracted me to Christianity in the first place—the loving companionship of

Christ. Thank you, A.B, my friend, for writing a needed book that will strengthen every believer at the nucleus of the Christian life.

Christian friend, nothing will transform or impact your life in a greater way than your personal time with Jesus. Nothing will impact your personal joy more than privately worshipping Jesus. Nothing will resolve your anxiety, change your demeanor, or magnify your Saviour better than the fruit that flows from personal devotion! Enjoy these pages, but most of all, rediscover the joy of knowing Jesus!

Venson I. Pugh, Senior Pastor

Reach For the Son Christian Fellowship

35 years of friendship with Bishop A.B. Vines

Introduction

Life, generally, can be challenging most times. Every one of us experiences those moments when it appears as though life doesn't make sense anymore. At those times, we feel that the entire world is collapsing on top of us. This position applies to everyone, irrespective of our different races, genders, social statuses, backgrounds, etc.

It is usually at those dark moments of our lives that the thought of committing suicide, giving up and engaging in one form of vice or the other, starts to find expression in the hearts of many people. The despair, depression, and hopelessness that come with these moments are usually overwhelming, thereby pushing many people into committing evils or giving up.

Different authors and writers, leaning on their various experiences from their fields of human endeavors, have tried so hard to proffer a lasting solution to this problem. However, all of these human approaches have only resulted in yielding little or no results in addressing the problems that we all face on our life's journey.

To provide a lasting solution to the challenges of life, it's very important that we fully understand the nature of man. Man, as God's creature, is a tripartite being. He is principally a spirit that has a soul and lives inside a body.

To overcome life's challenges and difficulties, one must first seek solutions from the realm of the spirit. Except for the spirit, man is saved, and the mind is renewed or transformed by the Word of God. No amount of human psychology, philosophies, ideologies, or clichés can help man overcome the turbulent moments of his life.

"Faith Moment," therefore, is a book written to inspire, encourage, and strengthen people during the dark moments of their lives. It also aims at helping people maximize their full potential here on earth by leveraging the word of God and other spiritual weapons as potent tools for doing so

The book is a collection of broadcast lessons from my Faith Moments Podcast, featuring various Bible verses. The book is written to build, inspire, and encourage people to overcome their life challenges and become everything that God has created them to be.

It's a book that anyone trusting God to unveil the secrets of knowing what to do when life seems not to make sense should endeavor to read. It provides insightful, inspirational, and biblical strategies that should be employed in order to overcome life's hard times.

A careful study and application of the valuable lessons in this book would, in no small way, help people to become everything that God has created them to be in life.

The Blessedness of Each Day

This is the day the Lord has made. We will rejoice and be glad in it. Please, Lord, please save us. Please, Lord, please give us success. Bless the one who comes in the name of the Lord. We bless you from the house of the Lord. Psalms 118:24-26 (NLT)

We serve a God who is good, merciful, and loving. It doesn't matter what we go through in the journey of life, we should always be

patient, celebrating each day with an attitude of gratitude, knowing fully well that God has designed each day for our utmost good and enjoyment.

As believers in Christ Jesus, we should be continually armed with the truth that we live in a passing world. "1 John 2:17 tells us, *"And the world is passing away, and the lust of it; but he who does the will of God abides forever."*

Everything that we see today, like the fine car, house, wife, children, and others, will surely pass away one day. Nothing on this earth is meant to last forever. Knowing this truth therefore, our attitude towards each day should be to live it to the fullest, expressing gratitude and appreciation to God for its arrival.

You see, every blessed day by God presents us with an opportunity to start all over again. Yes, we might have made some mistakes or had some drama in the past, but we shouldn't allow them to ruin our today. Instead, we should be thankful to God for every single day of our lives, utilizing new opportunities and chances that God brings to our way.

Let me quickly tell you this: each day of our lives comes with new blessings waiting for us to utilize them properly. If we continue to focus on the drama of the past, we will never maximize the opportunities of each brand-new day.

The right attitude that we should, therefore, maintain is to always welcome each day with thankfulness and gladness, not minding the bills we need to pay and the problems we have to solve.

You and I only have today to cherish because tomorrow is never promised. Since our future is uncertain or unknown, we should strive to fully embrace, maximize, and appreciate today. Truly, once today and its opportunities are gone, we will never recover or get it back again.

Remember this: you are the only one who has absolute and final control over your life's choices; no other person in this life does so. Therefore, use the opportunities wisely and productively. Always make sure that each day meaningfully counts in your life. The best way to do this is to ensure that you live your life to the fullest while also supporting those around you to do the same.

Be constantly thankful to God for the life, right relationships, good family, job opportunities, and other benefits that He has given to you. In fact, you have to be thankful for everything that God has blessed you with. If you sincerely count your blessings and name them one after the other, you will discover how good and gracious the Lord has been to you.

As I conclude this chapter, always remember that tomorrow is not guaranteed, and the best way to enjoy today is to be exceedingly grateful to God. You are a living miracle! Nothing in life could be compared to the miracle of waking up in sound health and mind each day. So, see every day of your life as a gift from God, and you will harness and maximize the numerous opportunities that come with it.

SELF-REFLECTIVE QUESTIONS

1)When you wake up each day, how do you approach the day ahead? What mindset or attitude do you intentionally bring to each new day in your life?

2)Are you finding yourself held back by past mistakes and regrets, making it a challenge to embrace new opportunities in the present?

3)Do you actively strive to make the most of each day, ensuring every moment is filled with meaning and purpose?

4)How do you ensure that you are making the most of today, acknowledging that tomorrow is uncertain and not guaranteed?

5)Are you making a deliberate effort to set aside time every day to reflect on and appreciate the blessings in your life, acknowledging and being grateful for each one?

The Brevity of Life

"So teach us to number our days, That we may cultivate and bring a heart of wisdom to You." Psalms 90:12 (AMP)

I will begin this chapter by reminding us that we all have limited time to spend here on earth as pilgrims.

This is one clear truth that some people have failed to understand and appropriate in their lives.

The number of our days here on earth is already known and determined by God. To properly maximize our few days here on the earth, it's highly imperative that we lay hold on these two words: Experience and Wisdom. First, an experience refers to something that you are going through or probably have gone through in your life. It's something that you are actively engaged in, the process of learning from your own actions.

Wisdom, on the other side, has to do with the acquisition of knowledge, understanding, and insight from other people's experiences. Experience is a school that every fool will attend, but wisdom has to do with the enrollment of people into the school every day.

It's a choice that you have to make as an individual to either go for experience and learn both the good and bad in it or to choose wisdom and come out better because you have learned from other people's mistakes. The choice is yours, but it would be highly profitable for you to go for the latter due to the shortness of life.

Beloved, be open and attentive to learn from other people. When you do that, it will help you to avoid the mistakes that others have already made in their lives. You move your life higher and faster when you go for wisdom rather than experience.

As an individual, I have the privilege of being a mentor to many people who submit under my mentorship. In such occasions, I expect my mentees to surpass me by going higher, shining brighter, and becoming better than I am. This is because they have the opportunity to learn from my past and present decisions, mistakes, and experiences.

I also encourage them to avoid making mistakes that I made in the past. There are five tips that I have carefully outlined on how to maximize the number of your days. Let's consider them individually.

1) Know Your Purpose and Live It: When the purpose of something is not known, abuse is highly inevitable. People who have not yet discovered their purpose of living, or who have discovered theirs but are not actively engaged in fulfilling it, are usually the ones that waste the number of their days on earth.

When people are not driven by a definite purpose in life, they allow or make room for life to drive them in any direction instead of exercising control over their lives. The result of this is that people tend to live their lives aimlessly and wastefully.

As for me, bishop, I already know my purpose here on earth. My purpose in life is to reach, equip, inspire, grow, and nurture (R.E.I.G.N.) others to fulfill their destinies in God. On a daily basis, I strive to spiritually, emotionally, and physically support God's people to lead impactful lives.

One of the most exciting things about discovering your purpose and living it out is that it brings a sense of fulfillment and satisfaction. Nothing on the entire earth, not even money or any other material possessions, could give you the feeling of achievement and satisfaction that living out your purpose brings.

Never assume that you know it all in the journey of life. Life is a learning ground, and you need to be a life-long learner so as to make full use of it. Those who fail to give themselves to continuous learning in life hardly ever make the most use of it. Learning is the key to meaningful growth in life!

One of the good things you can do for yourself in life is to surround yourself with good and experienced mentors who will propel you to become everything that God has destined or created you to be in life.

Of course, I do have mentors that I learn from in my journey of life. My mentors also have people from whom they can learn equally. At any stage you find yourself in life, there's always someone you can learn from or be under their mentorship. But by all means, try to avoid the "arrival mentality." It will only cause you to fade out mentally and quickly in life.

2) Build Meaningful Relationships That Bring Out the Best In You: Find and associate with people who would help to positively build you up in life. As much as possible, consciously avoid the path of those who would make you feel that every day is the worst day in your life. Wrong people or associations add to your drama or problems in life, so you don't have to associate with them. The best you can do for them is to intentionally keep them at arm's length.

3) Nurture Each Day as Though It Was Your Final Opportunity: Be more focused on your today's activities than on your tomorrow's achievements. This is because tomorrow is not promised or guaranteed. We only have today to live and enjoy.

Even Jesus, while He was teaching His disciples about the orderliness and priority of prayer, equally emphasized the need to nurture and live each day to the fullest. This is captured in verse eleven of Matthew chapter Six. The verse says, *"give us this day our daily bread."*

A primary reason we should focus only on today's task is because our life is likened to that of the grass and the glory of it, as the flower of the same grass. 1 Peter 1:24 says, *"All flesh is like grass and all its glory like the flower of grass."* The grass withers, and the flower falls off.

You are not assured of tomorrow, next week, next month, and next year because they have not yet been promised to you. This is the major reason I live each day with eternity in view. I don't know the particular time that I will leave this planet.

So, the secret of productive living lies in ensuring that you live your life to the fullest each day. This will help you to avoid the three regrets of *"I Should have...," "I Could have..." and "I Would have."*

4) Reach Out to Those Close to You for Meaningful Conversation and Reconnection: Learn to spend time with the people you love. As for me, I made it a deliberate act to always spend time with my family- my wife, children, and grandchildren. Take time to tell people that you love them. It breeds a sense of warmth, belonging, and confidence in them.

Reconnect with people and never allow social media to distract you from having meaningful connections. Don't channel or focus a substantial part of your life on liking, commenting, and sharing various posts on your social media handles.

Instead, reconnect with the real people in your life that you love or that would help to bring out the best in you.

5) Take Time for Self-Care and Relaxation: When necessary, try to get re-energized, refreshed and refocused. Doing this helps you to feel relaxed and become better equipped to carry out all the assignments that God wants you to do or has committed unto your hands.

If you keep yourself from being too busy, you will not burn out. So, sit down, relax, and find out what gives you joy. When you find it, be sure to engage in it. Learn to always engage in some self-care treatment, even during your busy schedules. *"It's a great tool for making the most of your time."*

SELF-REFLECTIVE QUESTIONS

1) In order to maximize your time on earth, what are the two essential things you believe one should hold on to? These could be tangible or intangible aspects that you consider crucial for making the most of your life.

2) What specific benefits do you think come from prioritizing wisdom over experience in life? How have you seen wisdom positively impact situations compared to relying solely on experience?

3) In your opinion, what do you believe should be the primary motivation for pursuing your purpose? Is it personal fulfillment, making a positive impact on others, leaving a legacy, or something else?

4) When it comes to learning and growth, do you actively seek out mentors to learn from, or do you believe that one can succeed without learning from others? What has been your experience with mentorship and learning from others?

5) How frequently do you engage in deep, meaningful conversations and make an effort to reconnect with those who are close to you? Can you share any specific ways in which these connections have enriched your life?

The Power of Your Tongue

Death and life are in the power of the tongue, and those who love it will eat its fruit. Proverbs 18:21 (NKJV)

Words are highly powerful. The very words that proceed out of your mouth have the capacity to either kill or give life, both to you as an individual as well as to others. As far as spoken words are concerned, you will definitely reap what you choose to invest in.

Galatians 6:7 says,

> *"Do not be deceived; God is not mocked; for whatever a man sows, that he will reap."*

It's very crucial, therefore, that you change how you see or view your world. This is because how you see your world affects other people's lives as well.

If you see your world from an optimistic lens, you will affect other people's lives positively. Conversely, if you see your life from a pessimistic lens, you will affect other people's lives negatively.

So, it's necessary that you become very careful of your daily vocabulary- the kinds of words that you speak on a daily basis. As you go about your daily activities, be intentional about the words that you allow to escape from your mouth because life and death are in them. Using positive and uplifting language requires a variety of skills; it is not something that people do ordinarily or naturally. You have to be deliberate, conscious, and consistent when using positive and uplifting language.

When you learn to use daily positive affirmations from the word of God, it helps you to start your day with joy and gladness. It will be highly advantageous for you to renew your mind on what and how you think because you are a product of your thought pattern. **"As he thinks in his heart, so he is"**- Proverbs 23:7.

Learn to appreciate every moment that God has given you. Don't forget that your moments easily turn out to become your memories in a minute. Personally, I have learned a long time ago to always appreciate and value every moment of my life. The reason is because they will soon turn out to be good memories for me.

FIVE THINGS THAT CAN REMIND YOU OF USING ENCOURAGING WORDS

1) Enhance Your Understanding and Wisdom with The Power of Encouraging Words: You can achieve this by engaging in a deeply personal study of some portions of the Bible that basically talk about the power and benefits of using the right and encouraging words.

Take, for instance, the book of Ephesians 4:29, which gives us a guide on the kinds of words that should proceed out of our mouths. It says, *"Let no corrupt word proceed out of your mouth, but what is good for necessary edification, that it may impart grace to the hearers."*

Studying and meditating on the above scriptural passage and other similar ones will help you to see and understand God's perspective on the importance and power of using encouraging words. It will also cause you to walk in a personal understanding of why you should be using them daily.

2) Empower And Guide Others Through Encouraging Words: Help people to build and understand the usefulness and the value of using encouraging words in their day-to-day conversation with others.

It's ideal to start your day by telling people "Great Morning" instead of "Good Morning". Yes, I encourage you to use the word "Great Morning"

rather than "Good Morning." Ordinarily, the order of arrangement of the adjective that is used to describe our day is- Bad, Good, and Great. My question to you is, "Why use or go for the word in the middle (Good), whereas the topmost one (Great) is available for you to make use of?" I would rather you choose the topmost one than the middle one.

It's better that you start from the top than from the middle when expressing your wish towards people on a daily basis. It's ideal to go in that order because, if by any chance, it fails to be a great day, it will end up being a good day". "Isn't that a better way to go?"

Use every possible way within your disposal to help others understand the huge benefits of using encouraging words. When people know it, they will begin to make proper use of it.

3) Celebrate God While Uplifting Those Around You with Encouraging Words: Learn to say things like these, "This is the day that the Lord has made, and I will be glad and rejoice in it," "I am fearfully and wonderfully made," "I am the apple of God's eye" and "I am blessed to be a blessing to other people." Learn to say them continually to yourself, as well as to others around you. When you learn this, you will experience a significant mental shift that will manifest in physical changes all around you.

4) Discover The Joy and Value of Using Encouraging Words: Don't just sit down and begin to complain about the bad things that are happening in your life. Instead, learn to live your life to the fullest, leaving out those things that you know you cannot change. Honestly, some days might be rough, but you can choose to see the good side of it. It's only when you do so that you can maximize them.

5) Release The Transformational: Teaching is one of the most pivotal and influential roles in life. Teachers, unarguably, are heroes. Without the presence and guidance of teachers in and around our lives, we would never be inspired to engage in profitable courses in life.

They help to teach, guide, and encourage you to achieve anything you want in life and go anywhere you wish to go or be.

Be apt to teach others, as well. Be the kind of teacher that brings out the very best in the lives of others. Tell people that what they stand to get from the difficult moments of their lives are valuable life lessons and not losses. Be the type of teacher who will always let people know that there is always something good to learn from their hard times.

THE IRREVOCABILITY OF YOUR WORDS

There is a unique and profound aspect to words. That particular aspect is that once words are spoken and released into the atmosphere, they cannot be erased or undone.

This characteristic highlights the consequential nature of our language and the impact it can have on others. Once your words have gone out of your mouth, you don't have control over it again.

Most times, people wish they could take their words back, but it's not usually possible to do so. This is a major reason you should think deeply before you talk. Desist from the habit of talking impulsively or reacting in anger. This attitude costs you much more than you could imagine.

Always take your time to critically and carefully ponder your words before you can go ahead and respond to any issue or behavior. As for me, I always try to choose my words carefully and wisely, especially when I am not in the right mood. Learn to do the same thing. It will greatly be of help to you.

SELF-REFLECTIVE QUESTIONS

1) When you approach life, do you typically have a more optimistic or pessimistic outlook on situations and events?

2) Do you make it a habit to start each day by reciting positive statements or affirmations to set the tone for your day?

3) In what specific ways do you actively engage with religious teachings on a daily basis in order to refresh and nourish your mind?

4) How do you actively encourage and guide others in using supportive and motivating language?

5) Can you share about a significant mentor or teacher in your life who plays a role in your personal growth and transformation through their guidance and teachings? 12) Do you think before you speak, especially when you are angry?

The Power of Encouragement

"Don't use foul or abusive language. Let everything you say be good and helpful so that your words will be an encouragement to those who hear them. And do not bring sorrow to God's Holy Spirit by the way you live. Remember, he has identified you as his own, guaranteeing that you will be saved on the day of redemption. Get rid of all bitterness, rage, anger, harsh

words, and slander, as well as all types of evil behavior."
Ephesians 4:29-31 (NLT)

E very one of us needs some words of encouragement at one point or the other in our lives. Therefore, be the person who is always ready to give them to others, much more than you expect them to do to you.

Don't form the habit of bringing other people down. Let everything you say be helpful and inspirational to the hearing of others. Be a big source of encouragement to people.

WHAT ARE THE BENEFITS OF ENCOURAGEMENT?

1) Encouragement Helps People To Discover Their Identity In Christ:

As a believer, you should be able to know your new identity in Christ. The new identity or nature is that you are fearfully and wonderfully made, you are the apple of God's eye, and you are blessed to be a blessing to other people.

These are some encouraging words that you can give to the people that you come in contact with every day. People need to know and be constantly reminded of their identity in Christ Jesus. This will help to instill the consciousness of who they are inside of them.

Aside from this, this mentality will also help them to refute satan's strategy of trying to remind them about their past life. Satan would always want to remind the people, especially believers, how unimportant they are before God or that they are not even children of God.

He always wants to identify you with your past so that you can forget who you are in Christ Jesus. Whenever he comes up with that strategy, constantly remind him whose own you are. Remind him that if any man is in Christ, he is a new creature, and old things have passed away. Remind him that Jesus has taken all your guilt and sorrows away while He was on the Cross. Always remember to remind him who you are in Christ because that's a potent way to ensure that he doesn't take you back to your old life.

2) Encouragement Reinforces the Right Things:

Encouragement stirs up a good attitude, mindset, actions, etc, in the lives of others. This good mindset makes them reason, behave, and act like Christ.

The Bible says,

"Let this mind be in you, which was also in Christ Jesus."- Philippians 2:5.

The mindset discussed here is a renewed and transformed one. Encouragement lets you know that no matter what goes on in your life right now, it shall pass away and be ultimately right for you.

3) Encouragement Inspires People in Tough Times: I don't know about you, but life is filled with many difficulties. Life, sometimes, could be challenging. The solution to life's challenges is to find hope, strength, and deliverance in God's word at those times.

God is who He is! His words are "Yes and Yes" and "No and No". Nothing on the entire earth can alter the words of His mouth. And in His word, He says you are blessed, that you are the head and not the tail, that you are the apple of His eyes, that you are blessed in your going out and coming in. When you meditate on these promises of God concerning you in your difficult times, they will help to strengthen, encourage, and inspire you to be stronger.

4) Encouragement Builds Spiritual Faithfulness in The Body of Christ: As believers in Christ Jesus, it's imperative that we build and encourage each other, especially in our lives' difficult moments.

I might not know what you are going through, but I believe God knows about it. He knows what you are facing right now, and He is more than enough to solve your challenges.

When we encourage each other in Christ Jesus as believers, we help relieve ourselves of some emotional pains and difficulties that we might be going through. 1 Thessalonians 5:11 (NLT) says, *"So encourage each other and build each other up, just as you are doing."*

Life, ordinarily, would have its difficult times, pains, and ups and downs. Sometimes, we don't understand what God is doing, but we should always be comforted that He loves us unconditionally-John 3:16.

When life hits us so hard, the best thing to do is to cling tightly to the word of God and not to clichés. Relying on God's word at such times will help strengthen, encourage, and inspire us to continue to forge ahead.

Isaiah 40: 30-31 (NLT) says,

"Even youths will become weak and tired, And young men will fall in exhaustion. But those who trust in the Lord will find new strength. They will soar high on wings like eagles. They will run and not grow weary. They will walk and not faint."

Beloved, you can have or do whatever you desire through Christ that strengthens you. Apostle Paul, speaking in Philippians 4:13, says, " I can do all things through Christ that strengthens me." I encourage you to never give up on God. Even when you have done all to stand, continue to stand.

Ephesians 6:13,

"Therefore take up the whole armor of God, that you may be able to withstand in the evil day, and having done all, to stand."

Continue to do good and never grow weary in doing it. When you stand, God stands with you. And when God stands with you, victory will ultimately be assured.

SELF-REFLECTIVE QUESTIONS

1) Do you tend to offer uplifting and motivating words to others, or do you often criticize and discourage them?

2) Are you someone who has a tendency to bring people's spirits down, or are you known for inspiring and lifting them up with your words?

3) Do you play a role in guiding and supporting others as they seek to understand and embrace their identity in Christ?

4) Are you proactive in using positive and encouraging language to reinforce and promote the right kind of behavior in others?

5) Do your words have the power to provide inspiration and strength to others, particularly during their low or challenging moments?

Attentiveness and Action on God's Word

"Understand this, my dear brothers and sisters: You must all be quick to listen, slow to speak, and slow to get angry. Human anger does not produce the righteousness God desires. So get rid of all the filth and evil in your lives, and humbly accept the word God has planted in

your hearts, for it has the power to save your souls."
James 1:19-21 (NLT)

D early beloved in Christ Jesus, I want you to know that life will throw its challenges at us daily. It does so to everybody; there's absolutely no exception.

The only way you will defeat or conquer the negative happenings of life around you is to know God's word. No matter how tight your schedules are, always find time each day to read God's word and have it stored inside of you.

I must be honest with you: If you don't have enough of God's word in you, you will certainly be overwhelmed by the problems of life when they arise. Remember, what I said is the Word of God, and not some motivational quotes or clichés.

It's only the words of the spirit- the Word of God, that can strengthen your inner man and give you the stamina you need to confront and conquer life's difficult times. No amount of sayings, clichés, or motivational quotes can do so.

You see, Jesus was able to overcome the temptations of the devil because He already had enough of God's word stored up inside of Him. Consider His responses to the devil in chapter four of the book of Matthew.

Matthew 4:4 *"It's written   "*

Matthew 4: 7, *"it's written   "*

Matthew 4: 10, *"It's written   "*

The devil would always come to challenge us, notwithstanding our standing and position in Christ Jesus. But the only way we can overcome him is by having enough of God's word inside of us. He only fears the WORD, not clichés, philosophies, and ideologies of man. The Word of God is the only antidote to the devil's attack.

Those who are wise give themselves to the wisdom of God. That wisdom of God is the Word of God. Inside of the Word is contained all the right tools that you need to conquer the enemy and challenging times.

You have to know that what you say or do daily affects the lives of others around you. So, when you have the right words in you, you will be able to change your life and that of others.

The Scripture is filled with various encouraging, hope-giving, and transforming words that you can use in your own life, as well as in the lives of others, for a positive outcome. I encourage you to make time to find, study, and meditate on them.

When you have these verses or portions of the Bible in your mind, and you release them to others at the right times, they will help to build them up. For example, Psalms 1, 23, 90:12, Philippians 4:8, 13, among other scriptural passages, should be stored up in you.

In every single day of our lives, God gives us ample opportunity to speak to others and to ourselves, as well. Be the person who utilizes every opportunity to encourage yourself and others.

Sometimes, you have to learn to encourage yourself continually in the Lord, just like King David did. This is because people are usually stingy when complimenting others. Be the number one fan of yourself by daily encouraging yourself using God's word.

Learn to speak words of truth to yourself, such as *"I am fearfully and wonderfully made," "I am the apple of God's eye," and "I am blessed to be a blessing to others"*. Constantly and consciously remember what God says about you in His Word.

Get the Word of God in your heart and let them stay there. This would save your life on many occasions.

SELF-REFLECTIVE QUESTIONS

1) Do you have a deep understanding of the teachings of God's word, enabling you to boldly confront the challenges in your life?

2) Do you prioritize and devote regular time each day to immerse yourself in the consistent study of God's word?

3) Is the direction of your life predominantly influenced by the wisdom imparted by God or by human/earthly wisdom?

4) Do you often draw strength and motivation from embracing the word of God within yourself, or do you primarily seek encouragement from others?

5) Do you consider yourself to be the primary encourager and supporter of your own life's journey, taking responsibility for your growth and well-being?

Don't Quit Yet!

"When you go through deep waters, I will be with you. When you go through rivers of difficulty, you will not drown. When you walk through the fire of oppression, you will not be burned up; the flames will not consume you. For I am the Lord, your God, the Holy One of Israel, your Savior. I gave Egypt as a ransom for your freedom; I gave Ethiopia and Seba in your place." Isaiah 43:2-3 (NLT).

M any times, when we go through life's challenges, we are tempted to think that we are alone. That's not true! You are not alone in the

journey of life. God has got you properly covered in your life's journey. When you go through deep waters- struggles, oppressions, and oppositions, know that God is with you. You are not alone; God has His eyes fixed on you in your difficult times.

Isaiah 43:2 tells us,

> *"When you go through deep waters, I will be with you. When you go through rivers of difficulty, you will not drown. When you walk through the fire of oppression, you will not be burned up; The flames will not consume you."*

I want you to know that you are not like anybody else. You have got somebody to shield and defend you from difficult moments of your life. His name is God, and He is waiting to lift you, even beyond your wildest expectations.

On our own, however, necessity is laid upon us to ensure that we lift God up at every moment of our lives. When He is lifted up in our conditions, He causes us not to get drowned in deep waters, as

His children. One thing about God is that He doesn't play with His name, especially when He is exalted and glorified.

Everything we have in life is from God, and when we give Him glory, He keeps us from drowning in deep waters.

Your oppression is a training ground for your obedience unto God. So, they will unfailingly come, but God has given you His promise that they will not consume you. Some things will definitely be difficult, but know that not all your oppressions came to rub you off your freedom.

In all things, learn to acknowledge God, and He will direct your paths. The book of Proverbs 3:6 (NKJV) says, *"In all your ways, acknowledge Him, and He will direct your path"*. Don't give up, don't quit yet! God is holding you tightly so that you won't dash your foot against the stone.

There are always some blessings on the other side of the road, but you need to go through deep- waters before you can access those blessings. It's in those difficult moments of your life that you will understand more about the workings of God in your life.

SELF-REFLECTIVE QUESTIONS

1) Are you frequently prone to comparing your life, accomplishments, and milestones with those of others? This might include aspects such as career success, personal relationships, or material possessions.

2) Are you often swayed or influenced by external pressures, whether they stem from societal expectations, cultural norms, or the opinions of others, even if they conflict with your own deeply held values, principles, or beliefs?

3) In your daily life, do you actively and authentically embody your unique individual identity, or do you find yourself feeling compelled to conform to external standards, norms, or expectations rather than expressing your true self?

4) Do you notice that you are more likely to be guided or influenced by observing the actions and choices of others, rather than being true to your genuine interests and deeply held convictions?

5) How would you assess your own sense of worth, significance, and value in comparison to how you believe God perceives and treasures you?

The Three Pillars of Life

"I will praise You, for I am fearfully and wonderfully made; Marvelous are Your works, And that my soul knows very well." Psalm 139:14(NKJV)

"He found him in a desert land And in the wasteland, a howling wilderness; He encircled him, He instructed him, He kept him as the apple of His eyes." Deuteronomy 32:10 (NKJV)

"I will make you a great nation; I will bless you And make your name great: And you shall be a blessing" Genesis 12:2 (NKJV).

There are certain times when life hits us so hard from every corner - right, left, and center. At those times, it usually appears as though the whole

world is collapsing upon us. The thoughts of despair, despondency, and depression that we encounter in our hearts at such moments are usually so unbearable.

To be honest with you, there was a time in my life when I found myself in such a condition. It was really a dark moment in my life. Life really hit me so hard that I had to ask God to show me what was going on in my life. I did exactly the same thing that Job did in the Bible when he was befallen by the trials of life.

It was at that moment that the spirit of the living God spoke in my life. In response to my question, He gave me three verses from the Bible. Since then, these powerful verses have been my lifeline. I can't help but continue to use them every single day of my life.

I decisively call them three pillars of life. This is because of their importance in my everyday life activities. Personally, I don't get out of my bed every morning without saying them to myself.

I am going to reveal to you these scriptural pillars of life that changed my entire existence. I encourage you to say them to yourself daily, especially as you get up from your bed every single morning.

You see, you need to have these verses permanently engraved in your heart because we live in a world of adversities and unbearable challenges. These extremities, most times, affect us emotionally and otherwise.

In my pursuit for guidance from the Lord about my current state, I received a profound message. The message resonated with the instruction to perceive me through God's eyes and not my own.

Before the revelation, I frequently found myself comparing my lack of progress with the success of others, which only served to amplify my sense of immobility. I was constantly questioning God in my heart why He didn't bless me.

In response to my worries, God gave me the three verses of the Bible that I talked about. He showed me the thought processes that I should avoid by gaining apt insight into these verses. "Here are the three truths that God showed His view of ME."

1) First, God Showed Me His Perception of Me. To support this, God took me to Psalm 139:14. The verse reads, *"I will praise You (God) for I am fearfully and wonderfully made; Marvelous are Your works, And that my soul knows very well."*

By the above verse of the Bible, I clearly understood that it is my duty to praise the Lord because I am fearfully and wonderfully made. You and I are God's marvelous work. We are wonderfully exceptional!

Our problem, however, is that we don't see and regard ourselves the same way that God sees and regards us. We often allow the outside voice to choke up or quench our inner voice.

Our inner voice is the spirit or voice of God that is within us. This voice always reminds us of who and whose we are. Our inner voice tells us how fearfully and wonderfully God has made us. It tells us that we were originally made by God for a unique assignment here on earth.

The outer voice, contrarily, wants us to believe the lies and deceptions of the devil that we are valueless before the eyes of God. This voice tries to make us see ourselves as less than whom God has created us to be.

It's your responsibility to learn to allow your inner voice to speak louder than the outside one, which is always telling you who you are not. When the Lord opened my eyes of understanding to this verse of the Bible, I immediately learned to stop comparing my life with that of another person.

I understood that I was an original version of myself. There's no need to try to be a copycat. As for me, A. B. Vines, "I strive to become the most authentic and extraordinary version of myself." All I want to do is to embrace the reality that I am a divine original made by God. I don't want to be a good photocopy of someone else. So, in the same way, I encourage you to stop comparing extremities.

2) Secondly, God Showed Me His Perspective Of Me: To confirm this as well, God gave me Deuteronomy 32:10. The verse says, *"He found him in a desert land And in the wasteland a howling wilderness; He encircled him, He instructed him, He kept him as the apple of His eyes."*

When you try to be extreme, chances are high that you may find yourself in a desert lane. Whenever you try to do many things simultaneously, you put yourself in a deserted place just because others are trying to do so.

I want you to know this when you learn to trust God in your struggles. Even despite your issues and hang-ups, YOU are treasured by God. That means God has me so close that He can see me in His eye. What a comforting thought to know the Lord sees His people this way.

Be encouraged that the Lord uses every desert, wasteland, and howling place to prepare you for what he has in store for you. He is always preparing a table before you in the presence of your enemies because you are the apple of His eyes.

You are so dear and precious to God, beloved. He watches you daily as you go about your daily activities. He is always filled with smiles and joy watching you because He loves, protects, and cares for you.

3) Thirdly, God Showed Me His Promise of Me: Again, the Lord took me to Genesis 12:2 to support the third point He told me. The verse reads: *"I will make you a great nation; I will bless and make your name great; And you shall be a blessing."*

I want you to know this: You are destined to be a blessing to this world. The Lord declares that you will be blessed to be a blessing to others. Yes, YOU will bless your family, friends, and community. I said God, wait a minute; the other two were excellent, but slow down. Don't you know I have learning disabilities and a speech impediment? How am I going to bless anyone? The Lord spoke loudly and clearly: I know who you are. I made you this way to get the glory through your life!!

I could never imagine this reality in the flesh as my mind wrestled with life's difficulties. Yet, in the depths of my darkest moments, a gentle whisper from the divine touched my soul.

Beloved, His voice will speak in your moments of vulnerability; surrender to God's unfailing love, and His unwavering power will prevail." These words resonated within me, echoing the wisdom of the Apostle Paul, who professed, *"For when I am weak, then I am strong"* (2 Corinthians 12:10).

This profound truth not only uplifts my spirit but also fuels my courage, which gives me the audacity to write this book. And I tell you with a clear and sound truth that YOU are fearfully and wonderfully made," and YOU are the Apple of God's eye, and "YOU are blessed to a blessing!

SELF-REFLECTIVE QUESTIONS

1) Do you view the obstacles and challenges that you face in your life as opportunities to grow and move forward toward achieving your full potential and greatness?

2) Do you believe that the challenges and difficulties you encounter in life are there to bring you down and hinder your progress?

3) When facing tough times, do you strive to learn from the experiences and possibly even endure losses in order to grow and develop as a person?

4) When you encounter challenges, do you consider yourself to have emerged victorious, regardless of the outcome?

5) Do you hold the belief that you have the ability to achieve victory in various aspects of your life despite the challenges that may come your way?

How to Have a Great Day

Understand this, my dear brothers and sisters: You must be quick to listen, slow to speak, and slow to get angry. James 1:19 (NLT).

1) Be Quick to Listen:

A lot of us are quick to talk without listening. Be slow to speak, even when you know what to say and how to say it. Learn to listen to people when they are talking, and after that, take some moments to digest whatever they have said before giving out your own response or reaction.

When you learn and apply this secret, I bet you will have a great day. This is because listening to others helps them get some relief from whatever they are going through in their lives. Consequently, you can't help others to feel better without doing the same way in your life.

When people are going through some difficult moments in their lives, all they crave is to meet someone who will grant them listening ears. What is in their hearts is to find someone they can trust and confide in, all they are facing. Be that person that other people would always feel free and safe to confide in them concerning what they are going through.

2) Learn to Believe:

And it is impossible to please God without faith. Anyone
who wants to come to him must believe that God exists

and that He rewards those who sincerely seek him.
Hebrew 11:6 (NLT)

Make it a point of duty every single day of your life to believe in what the WORD Of GOD says concerning you. It's what the WORD says about you that matters the most, not what the world is saying about you. "And what does the WORD say about you?" The WORD says that you are fearfully and wonderfully made, that you are the apple of God's eyes, that you are blessed to be a blessing to others, that you are the head and not the tail, and that God is with you.

Just imagine how great your day would be if you would learn to believe in these beautiful scriptural passages. The Word of God is ageless. It doesn't fade away, but the world's voice does. Learn to believe only in those things the WORD says concerning you.

3) Be Quick to Repent:

People who conceal their sins will not prosper, but if they confess and turn away from them, they will receive mercy. Proverbs 28:13 (NLT).

As we go through each day, we are bound to make some mistakes. We might have a great day, but never a perfect one. As long as we are still putting on or wearing this flesh, we will never attain perfection, no matter how hard we strive for it.

So, whenever we find ourselves engulfed in one mistake or another, the best thing should be to confess our faults to the Lord and ask Him for His mercy and forgiveness. We should be quick to repent from our wrongs.

If you will come before the Lord daily, repenting from your sins and asking Him for mercies, His grace will cover you up. Only when we conceal our wrongful acts and make allowances for their continuous commission will the Lord be helpless in covering us up.

4) Be Quick to Forgive:

Make allowances for each other's faults, and forgive anyone who offends you. Remember, the Lord forgave you, so you must forgive others. Colossians 3:13 (NLT)

Forgiving other people of their wrongful acts towards us is one of the most difficult things that we can do in life. But look at what the Bible tells us to do, *"Make allowances for each other's faults, and forgive anyone who offends you"*. Colossians 3:13(a).

Many people, including believers, still find it challenging to let go of some offenses committed against them a long time ago. They still remember some hurtful and unkind words said to them in the past.

Let me tell you one dangerous consequence of allowing the root of unforgiveness to stay in your heart: it makes you lock yourself up in a self-made prison of your heart and mind.

Forgiving others of their wrongdoings towards you has two double effects. First, it unlocks you from the prison that you have put yourself into. Secondly, it frees the person from where you have locked them in your mind or heart.

You are the major beneficiary of your decision to walk in forgiveness toward others. You set yourself free from sorrow and anguish when you forgive others.

Unforgiveness is just like a big load around somebody's neck that they put there themselves.

It's because of the huge benefits that are attached to forgiveness that the Bible reminds us of the need to forgive others at all times.

Matthew 18: 21-22, *"Then Peter came to Him and said, "Lord, how often shall my brother sin against me and I will forgive him? Up to seven times?" Jesus said to him, "I do not say to you up to seven times, but up to seventy times seven."*

Another good thing about walking in forgiveness is that when we forgive others, God, in return, forgives us of our sins. That is to say, God is extremely willing to forgive us when we forgive others and let go of unrealistic expectations - Matthew 6:12.

Finally, unforgiveness causes you to give someone an important place in your mind. This is a position or place that you should have used to think better thoughts and act wisely. By all means, learn to forgive and let go of all wrongful acts done against you if you desire to have a great day.

SELF-REFLECTIVE QUESTIONS

1) Do you often catch yourself eagerly jumping in to voice your thoughts before pausing to hear out others and consider their perspectives?

2) Are you the kind of individual who extends a compassionate hand, providing solace and a safe space for others to open up, express their emotions, and share their innermost thoughts and feelings with you?

3) Do you find solace in embracing and living by the promises and teachings of God, relying on them as guiding principles that shape your daily experiences, decisions, and interactions?

4) Are you naturally inclined towards offering forgiveness and letting go of past grievances, or do you tend to hold onto resentment and grudges, finding it challenging to release negative emotions and move forward?

5) Have you ever wrestled with the weight of harbored resentment, finding it difficult to forgive someone and inadvertently holding them captive in your heart and mind, preventing yourself from experiencing true emotional freedom and peace?

The "Acts" of Dealing with People

Always be humble and gentle. Be patient with each other, making allowances for each other's faults because of your love. Ephesians 4:2 (NLT)

I know you must have heard of and possibly read a portion of the book of the Bible called "The Acts of The Apostle." However, this is not the same Act that I am referring to in this chapter.

My own "ACTS" is the acronym that I have developed as a guide on how to relate with people every day of your life. A deliberate or conscious application of this acronym will help you to maximize your relationship with others. Let's consider the full meaning of the acronym.

1) A- Allow People's Time for Love (Respond)

Everyone you see or know may not feel loved or have someone say to them, "Great Morning." Others, on the other hand, may not wake up in the morning with their minds staying on Jesus, while some may not even have Him in their life.

Some people you know or see daily do not expect "some smiles," "thank you," and "how was your day" from others. Therefore, allow people time for Love. Let them flow effortlessly from you to them daily.

Most people walk around without being acknowledged, appreciated, and valued, hoping to find someone who will do so for them. Let people know how amazing they are, and make them feel loved by telling them that they are fearfully and wonderfully made.

Remind people that they are the apple of God's eye and are blessed to be a blessing to others. Just watch the smiles that come on their faces as you do so!

2) C- Care for People Until They Change.

Don't be too quick to withdraw your gracious words and deeds from others because they are not showing any positive change or improvement.

I am fully aware of how challenging it usually appears when people resist changes despite our care and encouragement to them. We are often tempted to withdraw our care towards other people when we see that they are adamant about changes.

However, I want you to know that everyone does not respond to positive changes in the same way and within the same time frame. For some people, it will certainly take a longer time of caring, loving, and encouragement for you to see the good sides of them. While for some people, it will just happen so suddenly.

So, don't give up on your act of caring for others until they change. Your motivation should be until I begin to see the positive sides of this person, I will never withhold my caring and love towards them.

3) T- Take People as They Are, Not as You Are, OR As You Want Them to Be.

We often expect other people to behave or act according to our own standards and judgment. We can't get the desired change we want in the lives of others with this kind of attitude.

When we view others only through our own lens, it can have a profound impact on our thoughts and emotions. There are moments when we desire some particular behavior or qualities from others, shaping the way we engage with them. Nevertheless, it's possible to hold certain perceptions about people and still hold them dearly and exactly as they are. As a parent, there are certain positions and levels you might want your children to be in life, which they might not be now.

Even as that, their current places in life shouldn't make you care less about them. Your attitude, at such times, towards them shouldn't be hostile. Regardless of their current position, you still have to shower them with love. That's the only way to push them into the positions you want them to be.

I do tell the members of our church, New Seasons Church Members, that there are two churches I am pastoring. The first church is the one that is in my mind, while the second one is the congregation before me.

The church, in my mind, always seems more purposeful, polished, and passionate. However, the ones before me, which is my living reality, need much work and patience to bring out the best in them. Therefore, I need much prayer, work, strategic understanding, and tolerance to make the church before me align with the one that is in my mind.

This requires a significant amount of effort. However, as I continue to work on it, I consistently observe that the division between the two churches is narrowing every day. This method has greatly improved my relationship with the members of our church.

4) S- Serve People with The Spirit of The Lord

Everything we do in life is, and should be, all about God and not ourselves. We all are stewards or managers of God's resources here on earth. We own nothing on our own.

As faithful stewards, we will surely give an account of our stewardship one day before God. You should ask yourself, "How are you using your gifts, talents, skills, resources, and time to serve God and others?"

God purposefully and uniquely brought you here on earth for a specific assignment. He specifically designed you to be a conduit of life, channeling blessings to others, not to act as a dam. People need to see God through you.

Beloved, always have it at the back of your mind that you are not serving men but God. I know you might quickly ask, "How do I serve the God that I am not seeing?" The people that you are serving are God's own people. And when you serve His people, you indirectly serve Him as well.

> Matthew 25 23 (NKJV) *"His lord said to him, 'Well done, good and faithful servant; you have been faithful over a few things, I will make you ruler over many things. Enter into the joy of your lord."*

Remember, you can't hear the word "well done" unless you've done well! So, ensure to do well.

SELF-REFLECTIVE QUESTIONS

1) Do you intentionally dedicate time in your schedule to nurture and prioritize meaningful connections and expressions of love with the important people in your life?

2) Do you approach people with genuine acceptance, seeking to understand and appreciate their unique qualities and perspectives rather than projecting your biases and expectations onto them?

3) Do you strive to offer assistance and support to others with a compassionate and empathetic spirit, exemplifying the values of kindness and understanding?

4) How do you actively apply your innate talents, acquired skills, and available time to contribute to the well-being of others and fulfill your spiritual calling to serve God and your fellow human beings?

5) Are you intentional in living in a way that exemplifies the teachings and values of Christ, fostering a presence of love, compassion, and grace in your interactions with others?

Avoid the Pit of Anger

People With Understanding Control their anger; a hot temper shows great foolishness. Proverbs 14:29 (NLT).

Τhe Bible is so wise and unique. It's as relevant today as it was when God inspired men to write it over 3,000 years ago. No other book in the world has endured the test of time quite like the Word of God.

It remains vibrant and relevant, offering wisdom and guidance that transcends generations. Each time we delve into its pages, we find new insights and truths that resonate deeply within us, shaping our perspectives and enriching our lives in profound ways.

The Bible, in several portions of it, tries to warn believers to always desist from anger. As children of God, we shouldn't be given to anger and unnecessary provocations. Anger is never an attribute of God except when used to kick against wickedness and injustice.

To avoid falling into the pit of anger, there are three critical things that we should do whenever we are tempted to get frayed up in anger. Let's carefully consider them one after the other.

1) Don't Trust Your Emotions:

Always check your emotions because they could be unreliable most of the time. The question is, "How do you put your emotions under check?" It is done by ensuring that you first analyze any given circumstance properly, putting your emotions out of it, and getting a bigger and better perspective of what is going on before you act or respond.

Check your emotions often. Get a better picture and understand any given circumstance before you react or decide to make any move. If you do so, your chances of falling into the pit of anger will be minuscule.

2) Learn To Take a Step Away.

Deliberately make up your mind to focus on the good things in life. Whenever the devil wants to remind you of things that are not going well in your life, remind him of what you have or what is going well.

Let me remind you this: there are people who took their last breath recently in that community hospital of yours, but God allowed you to be alive today. No matter how rich or successful those people were, you are more important than them.

Look at what the Bible says in Ecclesiastes 9:4: *"But for him who is joined to all the living there is hope, for a living dog is better than a dead lion."* Looking around, you must see certain good things that God has given you. Those things are good enough to be appreciative of God.

The gift of life is one of such good things and even the greatest of it all. So, learn to focus on the good and great things that have happened to you. When you do that, you will be far from the pit of anger.

3) Connect with People That Give You Hope:

In life, you must avoid negative people. They are not supposed to be your friends because they drain your energy. Learn to take a walk away from these people.

Life is so unsure, highly unpredictable, and mysterious. Associate or hang out with people who live with their hope intact, people with a sense of hope and joy in them. Remember that no association ever leaves you the same way it met you. It either adds something good or bad to you or removes something good or bad from you.

One good thing about association is that you are the one to determine who comes within the circle of your friendship. Choose that circle wisely and judiciously.

Don't hang out with people who will bring you down or even discourage you because that's what life sometimes does. Instead, connect and reconnect with people of the same mentality; people who see hope in their lives, circumstances, and days.

Consciously, find people for whom you will invest hope, joy, and strength in their lives, and that will also ensure they invest the same godly virtues inside of you. Surround yourself with those who understand that without hope, you cannot do anything great in life.

Be a hope dealer. Help to encourage someone, giving them hope to live and be happy. Develop the habit of telling others that it will be alright no matter what they are going through.

Help people to see the bigger picture and how blessed they are, even in the midst of difficult moments of their lives. You will be far from the grip of anger when you do so.

SELF-REFLECTIVE QUESTIONS

1) When managing your emotions, what strategies do you employ to maintain a sense of balance and control?

2) Do you prefer to pause and gain a comprehensive understanding of a situation before responding, or do you tend to react instinctively?

3) In the face of challenges, how do you prevent negative thoughts and avoid the devil's schemes from clouding your focus on the positive aspects of your life?

4) Do you actively seek out individuals who inspire hope and positivity, fostering a sense of optimism in your interactions and experiences?

5) Reflecting on your social circle, who are the individuals you choose to surround yourself with as friends and confidants, and what qualities do they bring to your life?

Maintain an Attitude of Thankfulness

A cheerful look brings joy to the heart; good news makes for a good heart. Proverbs 15:30. (NLT)

We all are supposed to have some measure of thankfulness in our lives. The Bible says in the above verse that a cheerful look brings joy to the heart. This suggests how you, as a child of God, can change any gloomy atmosphere you enter by radiating and reflecting cheerfulness and thankfulness.

Agreeably, you might not be pleased with or like the nature of your job, business, etc, but keep that from getting you frustrated and taking away your cheerfulness.

Rather than yelling and scowling at everyone around you when your condition is bad, learn to be thankful. It would be more beneficial to you, as well as to those around you.

This is the day the Lord has made, and we will rejoice and be glad in it. If you start each day of your life knowing fully well that the Lord has designed this day for your joy, you will have every reason to be thankful.

When you learn to live with the attitude of thankfulness every single day of your life, there are certain things it will do in you. Let us consider some of the dividends of thankfulness.

1) Thankfulness Releases Stress.

I know that life might be difficult sometimes, with its ups and downs, all making you stressed out and depressed. "But guess what?" You can still be motivated by the fact that you are still here- alive and not dead.

God, by His special grace, still wants to use you. He still has some work He has kept for you and me to do here on earth. Because of this, be thankful to Him. When you choose to stay grateful in all life's circumstances, your stress level goes down.

Your mind is a powerful component of your entire being. What's in your mind can change your whole body. So, learn to have a cheerful heart at all times so that your body will be in proper shape and free from stress.

Know this: Your thankful outlook on life will change other people's lives, too. Good news also makes for a cheerful heart. Be thankful and wear a cheerful countenance all the time.

2) Thankfulness Builds Energy.

Remind and encourage yourself daily that today is the day the Lord has made and that you will rejoice and be glad in it. Doing this builds a lot of energy inside of you.

"Will there be struggles some days?" "Will there be issues and setbacks some days?" definitely yes! But in all these things, decide to be thankful to God for everything. Be thankful to God for each day, as you can never do it again in your life.

3) Thankfulness Provides a Time Of Reflection.

I don't know about you, but for me whenever I think of and remember where the Lord brought me from, I am always filled with thankfulness. The Lord, indeed, has been good to me.

I remembered when I was completely down, and the Lord energized me. I remember when I was seriously struggling in life, and God sent me light in my dark moment. I recalled when I couldn't make it, but God opened doors of opportunities for me.

You see, without an attitude of thankfulness in my life, I would not be able to remember those things the Lord did for me in the past. Thankfulness makes me remember those times when God stepped in on my case and took care of my family, brothers, children, etc.

When you thank God for your present condition, He steps into your affairs to change your circumstances for good. We all have conditions that tend to silence our thankfulness to God, but we don't allow it to be so.

Learn to be thankful in all circumstances and every day of your life, regardless of the nature of the problem that you are going through. The abundance of blessings in our lives far surpasses the scarcity of things we may feel are missing. So, don't allow what you don't have to quench your thankfulness over the things that you have.

Consider the enjoyable meals laid out on your table, the comforting shelter enclosing you, the fashionable clothes adorning your body, and the gift of clear sight you have been blessed with. In fact, there are so many things in our lives that should make us thankful. Never take those things for granted because many people are not privileged to have them.

If you look around truthfully, you will know that God has been so good to you despite whatever you are going through. Don't allow the world to dictate your attitude or make you walk in ungratefulness. This is the day the Lord has made specifically for you. Find reasons to be thankful to God in each day of your life.

4) Thankfulness Provides Us with Motivation.

Anytime I look back to see what God has done for me, it motivates me to know what He can do for me in the future.

Whenever I sit down to think about all the opportunities, moves, and breakthroughs that the Lord gave me in the past, I am always encouraged and motivated to keep on or to keep pushing in the face of turbulent moments of my life.

If God could make way for me when I was stumbling and stagnating at some point in my life, I am very much aware now that He will bless me even more. Nothing on earth could provide such strength and motivation to me.

Even in the presence of excruciating pains of life, be thankful to God. You have to do so because inside your pains are some valuable life lessons that you are meant to learn from.

Only some have such an opportunity that you have to learn from their difficult times. Be grateful for all things.

SELF-REFLECTIVE QUESTIONS

1) Do you make a conscious effort to maintain an attitude of thankfulness to God, even when facing significant challenges and obstacles in life?

2) Do you have the ability to positively influence and uplift others through the radiance of your physical appearance and inner beauty?

3) How often do you carve out dedicated time for deep reflection on the countless ways in which God has shown kindness and favor towards you in your life?

4) Do you find it difficult to remain grateful to God when you focus on the things you desire but have not yet attained?

5) What specific strategies or sources of inspiration do you rely on to find motivation and strength during tough or trying times?

Winning Spiritual Warfare

"Put on all of God's armor so that you will be able to stand firm against all strategies of the devil. For we are not fighting against flesh- and- blood enemies, but against evil rulers and authorities of the unseen world, against mighty powers in this dark world, and against evil spirits in the heavenly places. Therefore, put on every piece of God's armor so you will be able to resist

the enemy in the time of evil. Then, after the battle, you will still be standing firm". Ephesians 6: 11-13(NLT)

L ife is a battlefield and not a playing ground. I don't mean physical battles that are fought with guns, knives, and other physical weapons. However, this is spiritual war, and it is only those who have a mastery of spiritual weapons that can win.

In our daily lives, we often tend to forget that we are in a battle or spiritual warfare against the forces of darkness. The devil, since he was cast out of heaven, has only one desire. That desire is to bring you down and snatch your soul away from your Maker because he knows that YOU are fearfully wonderfully made, that YOU are the apple of God's eyes, and that YOU are blessed to be a blessing.

If he is unable to bring you down because of your redemptive position in Christ Jesus, he will try to make you lose your testimonies and witness. Some believers are often quick to lose consciousness of who they are in Christ Jesus.

When this happens, they forget their situation and cling to their circumstances. They lose sight of the fact that their situation remains unchangeable while their circumstances change or fluctuate.

There is a big difference between your situation and your circumstances as a child of God. Your situation is the unchangeable truth that you are a child of God. Because of your salvation, God gave birth to you through Christ Jesus. Nothing on earth can change that situation.

Inside your situation, however, comes your circumstances. Despite being a child of God, you will still face or experience some negative happenings in your life. Those trials and temptations that come to you based on your "situation" as a child of God are your circumstances.

Quite often, we forget that our situation is more substantial than our circumstances. We quickly yield to them and forget who we are in Christ Jesus, allowing our circumstances to conquer our situation.

The devil loves it when we lose our testimony and witness. His effective strategy is to make us forget our situation- who we are in Christ Jesus- and be consumed by our circumstances.

See, one danger of forgetting who you are in Christ Jesus as a result of your circumstances is that it makes you return to who you were before you accepted Jesus Christ as your Lord and Personal Savior.

You might have all kinds of unfortunate things when you were not in Christ Jesus, but not now again. By your salvation experience, old things have passed away, and behold, all things have become new. In Christ Jesus, you have shifted your position from darkness to light. 2 Corinthians 5:17.

Beloved, you have to recognize that you are on a battlefield. Your opponent is the enemy. You see, when someone comes at you physically to either attack or harm you, don't take it lightly. Always know that there's a spirit that prompted their actions towards you.

The devil can be very crafty in executing his evil deeds against you. He can use one moment of your lack of discreet judgment to destroy your decades of faithfulness. That's a major reason you have to be strong in the Lord every single day of your life.

To withstand this battle with the enemy, you need to spend quality time with Jesus. You can only defeat him by leveraging on the spiritual weapons available to you as a believer. By using the tools of daily devotion, prayer, fasting, worship, and others, you can defeat him.

You have to constantly pray to God to help you detect the guiles of the enemy. You must also remind him- the devil, that you are fearfully and wonderfully made, who you are, and where you are going in life. Remind him of your purpose and destiny in God.

When the devil throws the weapon of discouragement and depression at you, learn to refute it by engaging the spiritual weapon of prayers and the other armor of God. That's the only way you can fight and win.

SELF-REFLECTIVE QUESTIONS

1) Are you conscious of your identity and the significance of being a follower of Christ? Do you understand the depth of who you are in Christ and how it impacts your life and actions?

2) Do you allow challenging situations and external factors to overpower your perspective and influence your decision-making process? How do you maintain a balanced outlook in the face of adversity?

3) In what ways do you ensure consistent and meaningful engagement with Jesus in your daily life? How do you integrate prayer, scripture study, fasting, and other spiritual practices into your routine to nourish your relationship with Him?

4) When faced with spiritual attack or temptation, how do you actively assert your identity and authority in Christ? What specific scriptures, affirmations, or practices do you use to remind yourself and the enemy of your position in Christ?

5) How do you proactively address and combat episodes of depression that may be influenced by spiritual or emotional warfare? What strategies, resources, or support systems do you utilize to counter and overcome the impact of these attacks on your mental and emotional well-being?

The Happiness of the World Versus the Joy of the Lord

The thief comes only in order to steal and kill and destroy. I came that they may have and enjoy life, and have it in abundance to the full, till it overflows. John 10:10 (AMP)

S atan has three major assignments in the life of a believer. That is, he came to steal your faith, kill your joy, and destroy your destiny. It's your responsibility to ensure he fails in doing that to you.

Jesus, however, came to give you everlasting life. When we talk about eternal life, we are talking about a life full of quality, a life full of durability, and an everlasting life, the endless kind of life.

"How does the devil achieve his purpose in the lives of the believers?" he does so by putting the spirit of doubt, hatred, and fear in their minds. He penetrates through these areas to take their minds and attention off the bigger picture of what God has for them.

When this happens, the believers usually put themselves in a position they are unfamiliar with. They become discouraged and frustrated.

I want to be honest with you: the devil doesn't have any joy and, therefore, can't give you one. The mistake some people make is to think that the only way they would have a good time is to have a worldly time- going to the club, attending parties, drinking, etc.

As children of God, we need to know that we are in the world but not of this world. We are kingdom citizens. Our joy is not found in the things of this world but in the eternal things or things of eternal value.

The lifestyle of drinking, clubbing, smoking, and attending parties to feel good shouldn't be traceable to us. Our joy is in the Holy

Ghost. Even when we eat and drink, it's for the glorification and honor of our God.

Oftentimes, satan makes believers walk in illusion by making them think that they are missing out a lot by not engaging in those worldly activities. He makes them believe they can find joy in the mundane things of life.

Hear this: True and everlasting joy can only be found in living for and pleasing Jesus with our lives. As a child of God, I have zero desire to drink, smoke, and club. My happiness and joy are not found in those things. Instead, they are found in pleasing the Lord with my entire life.

The best and most assuring way to have your good time is to have it in the Lord and not on worldly things. Never buy the idea from the devil that the church is killing or depriving you of not having a good time.

You are not missing anything at all by serving and living for God. Know that eternal life can only be found in Jesus. Invest your life and treasure mostly in the eternal things. That's what matters the most!

At the end of your life's journey, clubbing, smoking, drinking, and all of those things that you gave yourself as a means of having a good time wouldn't matter at all. What will be important is how you live your life.

It's the positive impact that you made in the lives of others that will undoubtedly be remembered and valued. Don't love the world at the expense of your eternal destiny.

As for me, I have made up my mind to invest my time in encouraging, inspiring, and making others fulfill their destinies in God. Find something that will make God smile and stick to it. Only by doing what pleases God can you have true joy and a good time.

SELF-REFLECTIVE QUESTIONS

1) Are you fully aware of the three primary assignments of the devil in your life, which may include temptation, deception, and division, aiming to lead you away from your faith and into darkness?

2) What activities or experiences do you consider as bringing genuine joy and fulfillment into your life, and how do you prioritize them in your daily routines?

3) As a citizen of the kingdom of God or an ambassador for Christ on earth, how do you strive to embody the values of love, compassion, and righteousness in your interactions with others and in the choices you make?

4) What specific aspects of your life, whether relationships, personal achievements, or spiritual growth, bring you the greatest sense of joy, contentment, and purpose?

5) Do you ever feel conflicted between pursuing worldly desires and serving God, and if so, how do you navigate this internal struggle in your daily life?

Maintain Spiritual Alertness

Stay alert! Watch out for your great enemy, the devil. He prowls around like a roaring lion, looking for someone to devour. Stand firm against him, and be strong in your faith. Remember that your family of believers all over the world is going through the same kind of suffering you are". 1 Peter 5:8-9 (NLT)

S atan's job, as we have repeatedly said, is to steal, kill and destroy. He doesn't have any good plans or intentions for anyone. Not at all! he is all set out for destructive plans, and his main target is the believers.

One powerful tool he frequently uses is "The tool of distraction." He orchestrates many distractions every day in our lives just to take our eyes and minds off the prize of becoming more and more like Jesus Christ.

Knowing this, therefore, we need to stay on alert against his strategies, plans, schemes, etc, that would cause us to lose sight of our pursuit because he is seriously out against us. He is eternally damned for ruining and wrecking our lives and precious destinies.

If we must maintain our focus and avoid his distractions, we must stand firm against him. Look at our anchor verse: "Stand firm against him." It didn't ask us to fight him but to stand strong in our faith. This means the battle is of the Lord, not ours.

We need to keep pushing forward spiritually because we don't wrestle against flesh and blood but against unseen forces of darkness. Sadly enough, too many of us do become victims of the devil's attack in this spiritual warfare because we are given to so many different things that bring distractions to our ways.

These distractions usually come to us through the news we hear or some recent happenings that come our way via our social media handles, televisions, and other channels of accessing information. When we pay attention to these happenings, unguardedly, it makes us lose consciousness of who and whose we are.

Beloved, I want you to know that we are battling with the enemy, and the devil wants you not to fulfill your destiny in God. He wants to deprive you of joy and peace that surpasses all human understanding in Christ Jesus.

Put enough things- words in your life that will cause you to look at the things of life versus life itself. Jesus said, *"I have come to give you life and life in abundance.* John 10:10(b).

Life doesn't consist in the amount of things that you have. Therefore, when you focus on the things of life and not life itself, you will most definitely be distracted by the things, and you will fail to enjoy the life that God has given you. When this happens, you get easily distracted.

You have to know that God is on your side, though it takes time and work to comprehend, most of the time. Coming to this realization would help you to be aware that what you are going through is not rubbing off on your destiny but could be developing you into becoming the best version of yourself.

The truth is, God's delay is never his denial. Your delay is meant for you to be developed into the best version of yourself. It is meant to make you the person that God has created you to become.

That's the major reason you have to stand firm during your trial periods.

Our God is so wise. Sometimes, He delays your blessings to develop you into a better person through your difficult times. Know that God is taking you on a journey of self-discovery and fulfillment. He is not and can never be against you.

The journey, most times, will cause you to suffer so that you can walk into your destiny, fully prepared to handle the blessings. The suffering doesn't respect your status, race, or continent. Everyone you see in life goes through one suffering or the other. There is no exception!

But you need to know that the suffering or challenge is to develop us. We might go through the shadows of death, impossible cases, and the rest, but we should always be encouraged that He is with us.

You are not alone in your fiery furnace. He is with you, so stand firm in your faith and in the glory of God. You will come out victoriously.

SELF-REFLECTIVE QUESTIONS

1) Have you taken the time to identify the specific distractions that hinder you from emulating the example set by Christ in your daily life?

2) Are you consistently vigilant and watchful, actively guarding yourself against the destructive schemes that the enemy may have planned against you?

3) Do you find yourself allocating more time and attention to information sources like television, radio, and social media platforms such as Facebook rather than immersing yourself in God's word and teachings?

4) Are you preoccupied with the pursuits of life, placing a greater emphasis on temporal matters rather than focusing on the essence and purpose of life itself?

5) Have you come to a deep realization of God's unwavering presence, understanding that He stands by your side even during the most challenging and trying times in your life?

6) How do you respond to the delays that you perceive as orchestrated by God in your journey through life?

7) Have you considered that God's apparent delays may be a deliberate process to equip and prepare you for a future that holds greater significance and promise?

The Faithfulness of God

"But the Lord is faithful; he will strengthen you and guard you from the evil one. And we are confident in the Lord that you are doing and will continue to do the things we commanded you. May the Lord lead your hearts into a full understanding and expression of the love of God and the patient endurance that comes from Christ." 2 Thessalonian 3:3-5 (NLT)

I want you to consider the first five words that begin the scriptural passages above. It says, "But the Lord is faithful". If there's anyone you can bank on their faithfulness at all times, it's no other person but God.

You have to understand that in your Christian journey, God will be faithful. I Peter 5:10 says, *"After you have suffered for a while," He will be your joy and strength."*

Unarguably, life could be difficult sometimes, but there's something good about knowing or having a good relationship with God. It helps you to pull through in such difficult times by giving you peace of mind that surpasses all understanding.

The faithfulness of our God towards us is unchangeable. Even when we are not faithful as humans, God has continued to be faithful and steadfast unto us. His faithfulness is seen and reflected in His various promises towards us.

His faithfulness towards us is that no weapon formed against us shall prosper; we will walk through the valley of the shadow of death, but we will remain unhurt; a thousand may fall at our right side, and ten thousand at our right hand; but it shall not come near us.

If you learn to trust God in difficult times, He will show up for you. Too many of us, truthfully, have not learned how to trust in

God. We pour our hearts to Him in prayer and still want things to be done in our own ways.

The Bible says we should ask according to His will, not according to ours. There are times when our "Will" conflicts with God's own "Will" for us. At those times, God might delay in coming through for us or even deny us what we ask Him for.

He does so because He knows that His "Will" concerning us is the best for us. He sees the better and bigger pictures of our lives than we do. So, the best thing we could do for ourselves is to learn to trust Him at all times.

God knows us better than we know ourselves. Sometimes, people are prompted to ask, "What am I praying for if He knows me better and knows what I want in life?". Yes, He knows because He is the Omniscient One. When we pray, we simply do so for the supernatural strength to be obedient to His Will and to hear His voice concerning His Will in our lives. Just keep praying for and in the Will of God for your life.

God is not and does not play gimmicks. Sometimes, life might put you in a difficult state that you may consider unfair. But know that God is faithful.

God is using your difficult times to mold you into the best version of yourself. Learn to trust Him.

The devil only came to kill, steal, and destroy. He normally does so through the lust of the flesh, the lust of the eyes, and the pride of life. That's why we should resist him through these areas of our lives.

1 John 2:15(NKJV) says, *"for all that is in the world- the lust of the flesh, the lust of the eyes, and the pride of life is not of the Father, but is of the world."* Satan uses these three things to destroy the lives of people. But in the midst of all his attempts to ruin our lives, God's faithfulness abounds towards us all the more.

God will guard and guide our paths when we get ourselves planted in His word because He is faithful. When you have some scriptural passages built inside of you, you will not be afraid of the challenges of life.

In His omniscient nature, He knows when to say, "Peace be Still," and everything in your life will maintain calmness.

He equally knows when you need to be pruned and walk through the valley of the shadow of death for His work and glory He has set before you. But in all these things happening around you, He is still faithful and will never leave or forsake you.

Whenever I can't see God's hand in my life, I trust His heart. Sometimes, I don't seem to understand what God is doing in my life, but I know that He is forever faithful.

Sometimes, I might feel like quitting or giving up, but whenever I remember His word and that He would make way for me in the wilderness, I am always encouraged to keep moving on. This is nothing but His faithfulness at work in my life.

You might be tired or weary about your life's current position-things might be falling apart all around you, your marriage might be at the point of crashing, you're about to lose or might have lost your job, but I beg you, don't give up on God. In the light of your current circumstances, I empathize with your struggles.

Despite this, I urge you to keep in mind and depend on His unwavering faithfulness, as He will guide you through these challenges.

SELF-REFLECTIVE QUESTIONS

1) Are you conscious of the unwavering faithfulness that God has shown towards you in your life's journey, especially during challenging times?

2) Are you willing to place your complete trust in God, believing that He will lead you to victory and deliverance during the most trying and difficult circumstances you may face?

3) What are the underlying motivations or driving forces behind your decision to engage in prayer? Is it a deep-rooted belief, a yearning for guidance, or a desire for inner peace?

4) Do you possess a solid foundation of scriptures and spiritual teachings that can empower you to stand firm and unyielding in the face of terrifying and daunting challenges that life may present?

5) Can you find reassurance and solace in the unshakeable belief that God's compassion and love are perpetually at work, even when the path forward may seem unclear, and His divine intervention isn't immediately apparent in your situation?

The Power of Humility

"So humble yourselves under the mighty power of God, and at the right time he will lift you up in honor. Give all your worries and cares to God, for he cares about you."
1 Peter 5: 6-7 (NLT)

O ne of the rarest human commodities today is humility. So, I beg you, be humble. Learn to humble yourself under the mighty power of God. If you learn to walk in humility, God will use you in a way that will blow your mind.

Walking in the spirit of humility helps you to learn from your surroundings. It helps you to grow because it is a pointer that you don't know all there is to know about life. One of the significant problems of our time is the "I know-it-all attitude." And this is nothing but the spirit of pride and arrogance at work.

Many people, including believers, are not humble; they claim to know it all. Nobody wants to hang out or associate with someone who is too full of themselves.

Everyone in life avoids the path of the proud.

If you are proud, you limit your potential in life. This is because nobody wants to hang out with someone with a haughty spirit. By doing so, proud people restrict themselves to many opportunities and possibilities that would have come their way.

Humility magnifies your strength. God wants to bless you, but you have to resist the spirit of pride and arrogance from taking root in you. James 4:6 (NKJV) *"But He gives more grace. Therefore, He says, "God resists the proud, But gives grace to the humble."*

God wants to bless you and blow your mind, but one of the ways He does this is through your act of humility.

Humility helps you to empower others to take the lead. A humble person gives other people the opportunity to grow and flourish.

Sometimes, you might be the best for a job or a given task, but you can allow another person to do it just to encourage them and increase their joy. This is precisely what the spirit of humility does.

The devil uses pride to destroy people. He does this by injecting the thought of superiority and importance into them, making them think they are better off than any other person in their given sphere of influence or environment. Pride makes you feel that you are the best in whatever you do.

As for me, there's nothing far more significant on the whole earth than seeing and helping other people rise and become successful in their different endeavors. As teammates in the body of Christ, we should help each other to grow to their full capacities. We can only realize this remarkable feat when we walk in humility.

God is very crazy about you. He knows your troubles, what you are going through, and where you are currently. But sometimes, He uses challenges to change us and pull us away from our comfort zones.

You have to learn to be comfortable in an uncomfortable circumstance. God, individually, cares so much about you. If He takes care of the birds in the air and the lilies in the field, He will certainly take good care of you.

As you go through difficult times, know that your delays are your pathways to progress and promotion in life. God is faithful and will turn every impossibility around you into possibilities.

SELF-REFLECTIVE QUESTIONS

1) Do you believe that it's extremely important to approach life with a mindset of humility, considering the needs and perspectives of others?

2) Have you ever found yourself holding back or not reaching your full potential in life due to feelings of pride and arrogance?

3) Are you willing to embrace the idea of opening yourself up to receive blessings from the Lord by actively resisting and overcoming the negative influence of pride in your life?

4) Do you find joy in assisting and empowering others to achieve success and fulfillment in their personal and professional lives?

5) Do you consciously cultivate a mindset of seeking growth and improvement, even in situations where you may be comfortable, in order to continue progressing in life?

Have a Mindset of Victory

For the Lord your God is going with you! He will fight for you against your enemies, and he will give you victory! Deuteronomy 20:4 (NLT)

W e are called to a victorious life in Christ Jesus, as believers. So, when you have a victorious mindset, you see the troubles and problems of life from a different perspective. You see them as stepping stones to your greatness.

As for me, I don't have losses in whatever I go through. I only have lessons, no matter how disturbing the circumstances might be. I know within me that the challenges that I am going through in life are lessons that God wants me to learn.

I see everything that happens in my life as a blessing that takes me to the destination or place that God wants me to go in life. I see the hand of God positioning me for greater heights in every ugly situation that I go through. That's what the mindset of victory is all about.

A mindset of Victory would ordinarily think in these directions:

1) I have Been Victorious: A person driven by the mindset of victory would always know that they have been victorious. They know that their past life doesn't define who they are currently.

These people are always aware of the many battles of the past from which God had delivered them. Based on this, they are fully convinced that if God could grant them victory in the past, He would even do much more in the future.

If you are quick to remember, you will recall that there were certain things in your life that you trusted God for in the time past that He did for you. If God could see you through, then it's an indicator that He will still do much more in the future. So, all you need to do is to have a victorious mindset in the midst of that storm of life.

2) I Can Be Victorious: We serve a God who never loses out in battles or wars. He is a God of victory. Whenever we are faced with the challenges of life, the best mindset to possess is that if I serve a victorious God, then I, too, can be victorious.

When you go through life's turbulent times, remind yourself that you can only get lessons and not losses out of them. Don't be too bothered about how people see you. Most of the time, what you think is a loss is usually a big-time win for you.

3) I Will Be Victorious: One significant trait of victorious believers is their steadfastness in the Lord. They are always assured that God can give them victory, regardless of the challenges that they are passing through.

Let me say this to you: You have to believe in your spirit that the God you serve is more than enough or able, and you can take care of what He says His word would do.

Even if you find yourself walking through the valley of the shadow of death, be strengthened that He is always at your side to grant you safety.

Remember this: With Him by your side, no challenge in life can overpower you. Therefore, consistently remind yourself that you will emerge victorious, no matter the circumstances of life.

4) I Choose To Be Victorious: Life is a product of choice. You have got to choose to make it on your mind, despite all odds. Choose to have a great day, a great marriage, a great business, great kids, etc.

I don't know about you, but I have chosen to be victorious in life, not minding the difficulties that I encounter on a daily basis. If you think victoriously, you will ultimately become victorious. If you're stuck in a cycle of negative thoughts, you'll give in to the struggles within your mind.

It's easy to get caught up in the chaos and confusion, feeling overwhelmed by the weight of your worries. But as I've learned, surrendering to the Lord's will provides a sense of peace and strength beyond measure.

You are a collection or summation of your thought patterns. The book of Proverbs 23:7 states, *"For as he thinketh in his heart, so he is"*. You can choose to think or be financially broke or not, joyful or sad. It all depends on the way you think.

Many people have the mindset of being broke, and that happens to be what they turn out to be.

You can be financially insufficient at the moment, but that doesn't make you financially broke.

You have to change your mindset and begin to think quality and Christ-like thoughts. Learn to think and act the way God sees you. What you think has a way of settling down in your mind or psyche. What you occupy your mind with determines what you experience in life. Choose to have a victorious mindset all the time.

SELF-REFLECTIVE QUESTIONS

1) Do you ever feel like you are isolated and on your own when you encounter the various challenges that life throws your way without the support or presence of others who understand what you are going through?

2) When you find yourself navigating through turbulent and difficult times, do you consciously turn to your faith and lift God up, seeking His support and guidance to see you through the challenges?

3) In your daily journey, do you make a conscious effort to prioritize acknowledging God's presence and seeking His wisdom as you make decisions and take steps forward in life?

4) Are you prepared to face and endure challenging and trying circumstances as a test of your faith and perseverance, recognizing that enduring difficult times can lead to the receipt of God's blessings and grace?

5) Have you found that the difficult and trying seasons in your life have provided you with a deeper understanding of God's purpose and workings in your life, offering insights and lessons that you might not have gained during easier times?

Reaping the Fruits of Your Labor

"Unlike the past, invaders will not take their houses and confiscate their vineyards. For my people will live as long as trees, And my chosen ones will have time to enjoy their hardwon gains. They will not work in vain, And their children will not be doomed to misfortune. For they are people blessed by the Lord, And their children, too, will be blessed. I will answer them before they even call to me. While they are still talking about their needs, I

will go ahead and answer their prayers! Isaiah 65:22-25 (NLT)

Any farmer that plants some seeds in the field does so with the intention of reaping some harvests in the future. The joy of every farmer is to reap the fruits of their labor. Unfortunately, some farmers fail to do so due to one issue or the other.

I know you might be going through many things in your life now. You might be losing your mind or thinking that everything is falling apart. The thought of hopelessness and despair might have saturated your life, making you contemplate giving up.

Before you do so, I have some strong words of encouragement for you today that would help to strengthen your mind and give you the hope to keep forging ahead.

God is directly speaking to you today through our anchor verse. He is saying, "My child, I know what you have gone through in the past times; I understand the losses you have recorded in the past, but I bring you better tidings." That good tidings is that you shall reap the fruits of your Labor. You are not going to labor in vain.

God is saying that invaders will no longer take your house and vineyards. The vineyards that the word of God is talking about here are your possessions. You will live as long as the tree and enjoy the fruits of your hands.

I know you might be going through some hard times, and the economy might not be favorable to you now. I am equally aware of the rumors of wars, the war itself, and other things happening today. But in all these negative happenings, His promise to you is that you will not work in vain. He has got you covered.

All you need to do is trust God during the entire process. When baked, a cake usually comes out scrumptious and delicious, but it wouldn't have been so if it didn't go through the heat process. So, the difficulties you are going through are part of God's training and pruning for your life. You will not be the only partaker of the benefits of the training that God is causing you to go through now. Your children shall be blessed tomorrow as a result of your perseverance today.

I don't care how bad the circumstances of your children are now, but all I know is that they shall be blessed. It takes fire to purify gold and heat to bake a cake or cook a meal. So also, it takes great pressure to bring out the best in you and your children.

When you see your children in a difficult moment, know that God is purifying them. He is trying to mold them into becoming the best version of themselves. You must learn to trust God in the process because He is their manufacturer.

You will reap the fruits of your labor. You might have labored in different areas of your life. For example, in the upbringing and training of your children, in your relationship with God and people, in your business, and others. I might not know what you have invested so much of your time, money, and energy on. All I want you to know is that your labor shall not be in vain.

No matter what you are going through, it's coming to pass, and your help is on the way. Hold on, endure like a good soldier, knowing He would make a way for you.

SELF-REFLECTIVE QUESTIONS

1) Have you contemplated the possibility of God transforming your current sorrows into moments of joy and blessings, turning your hardships into good tidings?

3) Have you ever pondered the idea of God bringing restoration to what was once lost or stolen from you, rejuvenating and replenishing what you thought was gone?

3) Do you have the unwavering faith to rely on God during the tough and trying times, trusting in His guidance and providence even in moments of adversity?

4) Have you considered that the challenges you face today might be a form of divine pruning, shaping, and refining you for a greater purpose in accordance with God's plan?

5) Do you realize that the trials you endure now could ultimately benefit your children as they witness firsthand the lessons and strength gained from the journey the Lord is leading you through today?

Value Relationship Above Service

"Jesus told him, "I am the way, the truth, and the life.
No one can come to the Father except through me." John
14:6 (NLT)

I want you to know this: At the end of our stay here on earth, the only thing that will matter is not our service to God, but our relationship with Jesus Christ.

Any work done in this kingdom without an absolute conviction and belief in the Lordship of our Lord Jesus Christ is a journey in futility. Such service will never benefit us, both in time and in eternity.

Without believing that God is authentic, that Jesus lived a sinless life, that He died on the Cross, and that He was conceived by the power of the Holy Ghost, every other thing you do in this kingdom is a futile experience.

You see, we focus most of the time on the peripherals, neglecting the center or the main thing. That center is Jesus. He is the only way, truth, and life. When you focus on Jesus, paying attention to what He says and does, He will show you the way to the Father.

During His earthly ministry, Jesus built a strong relationship with the Father, much more than He was engaged in His work for Him. He lived in an excellent Jewish way- He was always in the synagogue, gave his tithes regularly, and observed all the other Jewish practices.

However, He didn't just stop there; He went beyond that. The observance of the Jewish religious practices didn't affect His personal relationship with God, His Father.

Jesus should be the focus of our lives, not men or our service in His vineyard. The writer of Hebrew says, *"Looking unto Jesus, the author and finisher of our faith."* Hebrews 12:2(a) Only by following, truly and genuinely, the ways of Jesus can we be sure to come out of our difficult times. Beloved, in every condition of life, we find ourselves; let's have our anchor and focus on Jesus.

Focusing on Jesus wouldn't stop us from weeping sometimes in life. Weeping is part of the whole process. Jesus Himself had to weep at a point in His life when He came to the tomb of Lazarus.

In John 11:35, The Bible tells us that Jesus wept. However, we have to know that He didn't just stop at weeping. In verse 39 of the same chapter, He went further to order that the stone that was placed on Lazarus's tomb should be rolled away.

There are times in our lives that we are going to weep. But even at those times, we should never take our gaze off where Jesus is. Instead, we should learn to draw strength from Him and command every stone the devil has placed as a stumbling block on our paths to be rolled away.

We shouldn't allow the stone to continue to be a stumbling block to us because there is still some work that the Lord would want us to do for Him. There are many lives we need to touch. We are meant to transform many destinies.

We can not achieve some of these feats if we still have the stone placed on our way. I don't know the particular stone on your way, but I want to tell you to roll it away.

God has called you to do great work in your generation. You can't do so without rolling away your stone- obstacles on your journey. It's only when you have done so or wiped away your tears that God will use you to do great things. Receive the supernatural strength to remove the stone from your path in Jesus' name. Amen.

SELF-REFLECTIVE QUESTIONS

1) Have you ever taken the time to reflect on what will genuinely hold significance at the end of your journey on this earth, considering the impact you leave behind and the memories you create?

2) Are you driven by an unwavering sense of purpose and a profound commitment to serving in the kingdom of God, finding fulfillment in being a vessel of His grace and love?

3) Are you genuinely convinced by the truth of Jesus's sacrificial crucifixion and the profound belief that the Holy Spirit played a pivotal role in enabling His miraculous conception, shaping your faith and understanding of His divine nature?

4) Do you hold a deep and unwavering faith in the belief that Jesus is not only the exclusive path to salvation but also the embodiment of truth and the ultimate source of life, guiding your beliefs and values in every aspect of your journey?

5) Have you come to recognize that experiencing moments of sorrow and adversity is essential to your personal growth and development, fostering resilience, empathy, and a deeper understanding of yourself and the world around you?

He Lives Among Us

"For the Lord your God is living among you. He is a mighty savior. He will take delight in you with gladness. With his love, he will calm all your fears. He will rejoice over you with joyful songs." Zephaniah 3:17 (NLT)

G od is not just here but actively engaged in your condition. Never think that God is not involved in your challenges or in the midst of all you are going

through.

Don't think that He is not aware of your predicament; He's fully aware and involved in it.

When we go through some events in our lives, we often begin to think that we are the only ones going through such an experience and God has deserted us. No! He is actively involved in our condition.

You and I must realize that sometimes, God puts or allows certain things to come our way so that we can look up to Him. The Bible describes Him as a mighty Warrior and Savior. You have to be conscious of the fact that He lives among you.

God is a Mighty Savior. He is absolutely in love with you. That's why He sent His only begotten Son to die for you. Romans 5:8 (NKJV) says,

> *"But God demonstrates His love towards us, in that while we were yet sinners, Christ died for us."*

Never forget what God thinks about you. You are the apple of His eyes, created only for good works. He would calm down all your fears with His great love towards you. It might seem that you will not win, but He is telling you to calm down. You are going to win.

He is still on your side. Not just that alone, He is living actively among you, according to our anchor verse. On your side, you have just got to brighten up, knowing fully that He is there for you.

YOU are fearfully and wonderfully made," and YOU are the Apple of God's eye, and "YOU are blessed to a blessing! You have to walk in the spirit so that you can fully understand how God sees you.

So many times, we don't live our lives according to how God sees us. The ideal thing is to see ourselves the way God does. He sees you with abundance of life; He sees you as the apple of His eyes; He sees you making progress despite all odds; He sees you with gladness of joy. All you need to do is to cooperate with Him.

You might be in pain and sorrow, but I want you to know He understands you. The strength, endurance, and perseverance that you need to overcome your bad condition are in you because you are fearful and wonderfully made.

I want you to know that you are meant for this challenge. It's designed to bring out the best in you. Listen, you need to have fire and pressure to make something wonderful and amazing, something that lasts or can withstand the test of time.

You're not just ordinary. You can withstand this moment of your life because God put something in you that no one else can remove. He put resilience, perseverance, and courage inside of you to help you surmount certain challenges that life must bring.

God sings a beautiful song about you every day of your life. Part of the lyrics of that song is that you are His beloved and precious child. We all are members of His lovely family. There would be pain and joy, but if we persist, we would experience joy.

Get it rooted in your mind or heart daily that He is among you. He is your Mighty Savior. See yourself that He is with you. See yourself the way He sees and takes you.

Nothing on earth can separate you from His love. You can't lack because He is your shepherd. Stop worrying about tomorrow; God knows how to handle it for you. Learn to enjoy each day to the fullest.

SELF-REFLECTIVE QUESTIONS

1) Have you considered the possibility that God is actively involved in your current situation, working behind the scenes to guide and support you?

2) Have you ever thought that the challenges you face are meant to teach you to rely on and trust in God, strengthening your faith and character?

3) Do you make decisions and live your life based on spiritual guidance and principles, or are you driven by worldly desires and influences?

4) Have you embraced the idea of aligning your life with God's vision for you, seeking to live in accordance with His will and purpose?

5) Have you recognized that the obstacles and difficulties you encounter are opportunities for personal growth and development, pushing you to overcome limitations and become the best version of yourself?

Wisdom for Greatness

For by me (wisdom from God) your days will be multiplied, And years of life shall be increased. If you are wise, you are wise for yourself [for your own benefit]; If you scoff [thoughtlessly ridicule and disdain], you alone will pay the penalty." Proverbs 9: 11-12(AMP)

W isdom is principal in arriving at, as well as in, the maintenance of success in life. The wisdom that I am referring to here is the wisdom of God. It's not man's kind of wisdom that we acquire from reading any other book.

I am talking about the divine wisdom that is from God. God has given you the knowledge, wisdom, and blessings you need to become great. But first, you need to realize

that when you get wisdom from God, you also get guidance from Him. God's guidance helps you to maximize your wisdom fully.

God's word is a living and breathing tool meant to help you live each day to the fullest. It makes you believe in the bigger dreams concerning God's promises upon your life.

You must believe in greatness; it's God's design for you. Having God's word in your life allows you to live big or believe in greatness because His word is fully amazing.

Through God's wisdom, your days shall be multiplied. This does not mention addition, as in 1 plus 1 or 4 plus 4. No! It's talking about 5 times 5, 6 times 12, and so on.

I don't know about you, but I would love to live by multiplication. This is the true measurement of living great.

Beloved, I want you to listen to me. When you Learn to trust in the wisdom and guidance of God, the Lord says, "I would increase and multiply the number of your days."

I am not referring to the multiplication of materials things alone, like the cars in your garage. Instead, I am talking about the multiplication of things that matter most in life. Those are things that money cannot buy. Joy, peace, strength, and other things that are not bought with money.

I know there might be certain decisions we made in the past that lacked the wisdom of God. We shouldn't be concerned about them. When we partner with God, His grace covers us to make them right because He makes crooked paths straight.

The introductory part of verse 12 reads, "If you are wise…." This suggests that God always gives us conditions and not commands. It's a choice that we have to make and not a matter of compulsion. God is not a bully and can never be one. He always gives us the ability to choose whatever we want.

God can put specific cues before you, but it's left for you to choose which of the signs you are to follow. A sign is just a point in a direction on how we should go. God leaves us free to choose from many signs He places before us.

If you are wise, you will follow the right signs before you. And when you do so, you are still the one that will benefit from them.

Following the path of wisdom helps to keep you out of pain, positioning you in a place where God can bless you.

One good thing about God's blessings is that they are transgenerational. It has a trickle-down effect. That's to say, the generations after you also partake or benefit from the blessings. If God blesses me, He equally blesses my family, legacy, heritage, etc, that would come after me. But it all starts with you being wise and making the right decisions today.

I challenge you today to make the right choice by being a godly sign to your children. Never grow weary in doing so. You shall reap the benefits of your right choices in due season if you don't give up.

I tell you the truth, where I am today is largely attributed to the right choices that my grandmother made. My grandmother prayed for God to save and use her grandchildren. And today, I am a product of that prayer, inspiring and encouraging many people to fulfill their destinies in God.

Stay encouraged to make the right choices every day. You are not just storing blessings for yourself alone; generations after, you stand to benefit from them. God is equipping you with everything that you need to overcome the challenges.

You shall come out victoriously because YOU are fearfully and wonderfully made," and YOU are the Apple of God's eye, and "YOU are blessed to a blessing!

Congratulations!

SELF-REFLECTIVE QUESTIONS

1) When faced with life's twists, do you choose to navigate based on the profound wisdom attributed to the divine or rely solely on human logic?

2) Do you find solace and strength in embracing God's teachings as you navigate through the challenges of each day?

3) Have you ever considered the boundless potential for God to amplify your impact in ways that transcend human measurement?

4) In the midst of daily decisions, how intentional are you in recognizing and seizing the opportunities that align with God's divine plan?

5) Why do you believe it's crucial to walk steadfastly on the path illuminated by God's wisdom and grace?

6) Contemplate how the choices made today have the potential to shape and influence future generations, for better or for worse.

7) With a spirit of trust and resilience, do you hold the belief that you will overcome present challenges, paving the way for a life that is not only abundant but deeply fulfilling?

Made in the USA
Monee, IL
19 July 2025

21060059R00079